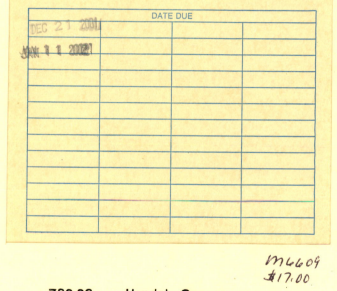

FOR STEVEN SCHOENBERG

diuites fieri in operibus bonis

GEORGE FRIDERIC HANDEL

MESSIAH

The Wordbook for the Oratorio

Words Selected from the Holy Scripture by Charles Jennens

Paintings by Barry Moser

Introduction by Christopher Hogwood

Willa Perlman Books
An Imprint of HarperCollinsPublishers

MESSIAH: THE WORDBOOK FOR THE ORATORIO
Text copyright © 1992 by HarperCollins Publishers
Introduction copyright © 1992 by Christopher Hogwood
Illustrations copyright © 1992 by Barry Moser
All rights reserved. Printed in the U.S.A.
1 2 3 4 5 6 7 8 9 10
FIRST EDITION

Library of Congress Cataloging-in-Publication Data
Handel, George Frideric, 1685–1759.
    [Messiah. Libretto]
  Messiah : the wordbook for the oratorio / George Frideric
Handel ; words selected from the Holy Scripture by Charles
Jennens ; introduction by Christopher Hogwood ; paintings by
Barry Moser.
    p.   cm.
  "Willa Perlman books."
  Libretto.
  Summary : An illustrated edition of the libretto for Handel's
popular choral work.
  ISBN 0-06-021779-0
  ISBN 0-06-021038-9 (ltd. ed.)
  1. Oratorios—Librettos—Juvenile literature. [1. Oratorios—
Librettos.] 1. Jennens, Charles, 1700-1773. II. Moser, Barry, ill.
III. Title.   91-21661
ML53.H14M3   1992 <Case>   CIP
782.23'026'8—dc20   AC MN

INTRODUCTION

FOR MANY MUSIC LOVERS, HANDEL'S *MESSIAH* IS TO ORATORIO WHAT *THE NUTCRACKER* is to ballet, an entertainment without which no Christmas is complete. *Messiah* is certainly more than music; it has achieved cult status as an icon of choral worship, and it often seems to have become more of a social ritual than a Christian experience. As listeners we are always audience, never congregation. Yet *Messiah* possesses to an extraordinary degree those two most disparate elements of art—spontaneous power and premeditated plan—that never fail to ignite more than mere musical enthusiasm.

Messiah is not a typical Handel oratorio; there are no named characters, as are usually found in Handel's settings of Old Testament stories, possibly to avoid charges of blasphemy. It is a meditation rather than a drama of personalities, lyrical in method; the narration of the story is carried on by implication, and there is no dialogue. In all this it is unlike German settings of the Passion story, and also unlike Handel's operatic techniques. He shows deliberate restraint in his choice of basic orchestral colors; there are no moments of solo instrumental display, other than the essential Last Trumpet. Very little of the text is set as simple recitative, but there is more than the usual quantity and variety of numbers for the chorus, which thus acts as the sounding board of the drama. This special scheme did not please all commentators of the time: "Though that grand entertainment is called an *Oratorio,*" wrote Dr. John Brown in 1763, "yet it is not *dramatic;* but properly a Collection of *Hymns* or *Anthems* drawn from the sacred Scriptures." This is not true; there is drama, but it unfolds in what has aptly been termed the "moral autobiography of man."

Credit for the compilation of this extraordinary text must be handed to the Reverend Charles Jennens, an outspoken and much maligned friend of Handel's. He was a wealthy country gentleman with a large estate at Gopsall, in Leicestershire, and an elegant London house in Queen's Square. In Jennens' correspondence with his life-long friend Edward Holdsworth, he clearly presented himself as the prime mover in the oratorio enterprise. On November 29, 1739, he wrote, "Handel says he will do nothing next Winter, but I hope I shall perswade him to set another Scripture Collection I have made for him, & perform it for his own benefit in Passion week.* I hope he will lay out his whole Genius & Skill upon it, that the Composition may excell all his former Compositions, as the Subject excells every other Subject. The Subject is Messiah...."

The overall structure of *Messiah,* like Handel's other English oratorios, is in three parts: Part I tells of the Nativity; Part II of the Passion, the Resurrection, and the subsequent spread of the

*Jennens had already supplied the texts for *Saul* and *Israel in Egypt.* He went on to supply the excellent libretto for *Belshazzar,* on which there is also a fascinating correspondence with Handel.

Gospel; Part III of the promise of Redemption and Eternal Life. The text is drawn from the King James Authorized Version of the Bible (1611) and from the earlier translation of the Psalms made for the Great Bible of 1539 and preserved in the Book of Common Prayer. This latter source gives us much of the Christmas text (from Isaiah and the Gospels) for Part I, while Part II uses the Services for Holy Week. Part III, with the exception of the final chorus, is taken entirely from the words of the Burial Service. It has been suggested that Handel himself may have added the text of "If God be for us." Certainly he knew the Scriptures; when it was once suggested to him that the archbishops might select texts for him to set as a Coronation Anthem, he replied witheringly, "I have read my Bible very well, and shall choose for myself."

In the *Messiah* text, however, many conflations, subtle contractions, and small alterations show the hand of a skilled librettist; Jennens knew how to assist the musical setting and the development of drama. His omissions from the full biblical text of the first aria (shown here in square brackets), for instance, make a repetitive statement into a picturesque and singable text: "Every valley shall be exalted, and every mountain and hill [shall be] made low: [and] the crooked [shall be made] straight, and the rough places plain" (Isaiah 40:4).

Proof of the identification of Christ as the Messiah promised in the Old Testament—the central doctrinal point of the oratorio—is offered by an alternation with texts from the New Testament.* This juxtaposition of verses from Old and New Testaments is most telling when prophecy and fulfillment are contained in the same musical number; thus "He shall feed his flock" leads directly into "Come unto Him" (originally "Me"). At the opening of Part III the words "I know that my Redeemer liveth" (from the Book of Job) lead directly into Saint Paul's "For now is Christ risen." So familiar are we with Jennens' sequence that it comes as something of a shock to find the disparate origins of verses we think of as one. Therefore the biblical references are included in this volume, although they were not printed in the original wordbooks including the 1743 copy upon which this volume is based. One imagines the public of the 1740s would have known their Bible well enough to identify the selections.

The worthiness of Jennens' text is proved by the fact that, although Handel over the years made changes to the music, he hardly ever felt the need to add or subtract a single word. Only one section of text was discarded: the end of the Duetto and Chorus version of "How beautiful are the Feet," which ended with a choral setting of "Break forth into joy." This was used in the first London performances in 1743 but then abandoned (possibly at Jennens' suggestion).

Handel's musical treatment reflects his concern that despite telling the story more by inference than narration, the pace should not falter. He opts for a minimum of *da capo* arias and a cumulation of varied numbers that, as at the end of Part II, can generate enormous excitement.

*From the Latin text which Jennens supplied to Handel as one of two quotes to print on the title page of the wordbook, we can see that "prophecy fulfilled" was his main theme; *majora canamus*—"Let us sing of greater things"—offered a reminder of what the Enlightenment liked to think of as proto-Christian writing—the *Aeneid* of Virgil.

His theatrical sensibility is everywhere apparent, not only in dramatic pacing but also in evocative symbolism and baroque "picture painting" in music. There were at first even more bars of trilling birdsong from the violins in the opening *ritornello* of "Every Valley" (Handel cut several bars from this music at an early stage); and there is the literalism of the rough places being made plain.

True to the theatrical manner, Handel includes typical set pieces from Italian opera in the solo writing of *Messiah*—a rage aria ("Why do the nations?"), a pastoral *siciliano* ("How beautiful are the Feet"), and a coloratura soprano showpiece with competing violins ("Rejoice greatly!") that would not have been out of place in any of his Italian operas.

Borrowing was a standard component of Handel's compositional technique. The nineteenth century felt special concern at the "immorality" of his appropriations, whereas today we incline more sympathetically to the eighteenth-century opinion that "He takes other men's pebbles and polishes them into diamonds." In *Messiah* he reused a number of his own secular compositions, especially a recently written set of Italian secular vocal duets. From this source comes most of the music of "And He shall purify," "His Yoke is easy," "All we, like Sheep," and other choral numbers.

Most of the borrowings can be explained—some would say excused—by haste of composition. The dates on the original manuscript that conclude each part show that, beginning on August 22, 1741, it took him seven, nine, and six days for the three parts, respectively, with a further two days for filling out the instrumentation; it was finished by September 14.

On November 18 Handel arrived in Dublin, at the invitation of the Lord Lieutenant, to direct a concert season in the Irish capital. He brought with him his new oratorio. The musical scene in Dublin was second only to that of London in activity and enthusiasm, and even the first public rehearsal of *Messiah*, on April 9, 1742, elicited from the *Dublin Journal* the report that it "was allowed by the greatest Judges to be the finest Composition of Musick that ever was heard." For the official premiere in the Musick-Hall in Fishamble Street on April 13, ladies were requested to come "without Hoops" and gentlemen without their swords, "as it will greatly encrease the Charity, by making Room for more company." Seven hundred people were reported to have crammed into the small space, and about £400 was raised for charity by "this Grand Performance."

Compared to such rapture in Ireland, Handel found the English public reception to the new work decidedly lukewarm when he returned to London the following season. Lord Shaftesbury recalled in his *Memoirs* that "partly from the Scruples, some Persons had entertained, against carrying on such a Performance in a Play House, and partly from not entering into the genius of the Composition, this Capital Composition, was but indifferently relish'd." Jennens also was less than overwhelmed by the work. On January 17, 1743, not yet having heard the oratorio, he declared to Holdsworth: "His Messiah has disappointed me, being set in great hast[e], tho' he said he would be a year about it, & make it the best of all his Compositions. I shall put no more Sacred Words into his hands, to be thus abus'd...." *Messiah* was revived for two performances in April 1745, but did not approach its later popularity until it was sung as a charity performance in 1750 for the Foundling Hospital, of which Handel was a Governor.

The wordbook for the Dublin performance was, as Jennens put it, "full of bulls"; there were many misprints, and one entire recitative was omitted. The librettist naturally laid the blame for this on the composer: "If he does not print a correct one here, I shall do it my Self, & perhaps tell him a piece of my mind by way of Preface."

Fortunately the wordbook was reset for the first London performances in 1743, and a recently discovered copy of this version (now in private hands) has been used as the basis for the text of this volume. In addition to dividing the oratorio into its familiar three parts, the 1743 wordbook is rare in that it uses Roman numerals to distinguish separate "scenes" within each part, although they are not named as such. This may well reflect Jennens' (or Handel's) own divisions, and certainly sheds new light on Handel's musical sequences and their dramatic implications (for instance the change of scene before "He was cut off" and the surprisingly disparate lengths of the two scenes that open Part II). The *Pifa* is not listed in the 1743 wordbook, and the arias are not allocated to specific voices.

While this volume follows the 1743 wordbook in all of the above, there are variations in some instances. It titles "Lift up your heads" as a "semi-chorus," which not only reflects the antiphonal style of writing, but may also be a residue of one of Jennens' suggestions to set it as an eight-part double chorus. However, Handel chose instead to alternate question and answer between the upper and lower voices of the chorus, and it appears in this volume as "chorus."

Other variants will be noticed that may lead to speculation on the niceties of Handel's compositional techniques, vagaries of eighteenth-century spelling or simply eighteenth-century lack of interest in standardization. "Burden," for example, was spelled by Handel as "burthen," and he streamlined "Blessing, and Honour, and Glory, and Power" by omitting the second "and." "And on Earth Peace" became "and Peace on Earth," and in the final chorus of Part I Handel removed the first word of "For his Yoke is easy"—possibly to fit his pre-existing music more easily. In the Passion choruses, the text of "and with his stripes" is simply a continuation of "Surely He hath borne our Griefs." However, it is separately titled in this version to represent the familiar triptych of choruses.

In other cases the 1743 wordbook is our guide to those sections of *Messiah* which were still undergoing experimentation. The text of "And lo, an Angel of the Lord," described in the 1743 wordbook as "song," later becomes "And lo, the Angel…" in the accompanied recitative usually heard today. But Handel produced an alternative and longer version, an arioso with continuo only, which was heard at the first London performance in 1743 but then replaced. "Their sound is gone out," a text that was not performed in Dublin, first appears in 1743 as a "song" for solo voice and continuo, and only thereafter as a chorus.

Later adaptations by Handel were almost all made to accommodate new soloists or to expedite the drama. One chorus, "Break forth into joy," which followed "How beautiful are the Feet," was scrapped to allow the more dramatically useful "Their sound is gone out" to stand as a chorus without competition; there was a risk of tedium with so many jubilant choruses to come. Handel dithered for several years over the right length for the *Pifa,* eventually coming to prefer the short ten-measure version, which sets the atmosphere without holding up the Christmas story.

In numbers of performers, Handel's demands in *Messiah* were more modest than most twentieth-century performances would lead the listener to suppose. He called for an orchestra of strings and continuo (usually harpsichord and organ), with oboes and bassoons doubling the strings and very occasional use of trumpets and drums. The surviving accounts from 1754 show that a typical orchestral disposition would have consisted of the following instruments: eight first violins, six second violins, five violas, three cellos, two double basses, four oboes, four bassoons, two trumpets, timpani, and keyboard continuo (harpsichord and organ). The number of soloists might be the typical four but could also be expanded with a second soprano, a boy treble, and a choice of male and female altos. For chorus Handel always used male voices—treble voices on the top line, countertenors for the alto—and assumed that the soloists would also sing in the choral numbers.

When he had larger forces for *Solomon* in 1749, Handel marked many sections in *Messiah* to be played *senza ripieni,* that is without the extra players. He did not expect any string solos—in fact no solos at all except the Last Trumpet. Later generations have indulged in gratuitous amplification of Handel's specific intentions on the "might makes right" principle. Such travesties can still be encountered all too frequently today and cannot be justified on any other than social or therapeutic grounds.

Time has proved *Messiah* to be immortal but open to every vagary of interpretation. It has survived all indignities of amputation, truncation, and reorchestration, the use of elephantine forces and Wagnerian delivery—even the foolish ritual of standing during, rather than after, the "Hallelujah" chorus, a habit that was first noted in the nineteenth century and has nothing to do with Handel. For any modern performer, amateur or professional, who takes an interest in Handel's intentions and vision, the best practical advice is to make use of a text, both verbal and musical, that represents his unadulterated intentions (but still offers his alternatives) and to approach the historical evidence with common sense and a faith in Handel's creation and the text that inspired it.

Armed with the same advice, audiences should find themselves in agreement annually with the critic of the first *Messiah* performance, who discovered that "The Sublime, the Grand, and the Tender, adapted to the most elevated, majestick and moving Words, conspired to transport and charm the ravished Heart and Ear" (Faulkner's *Dublin Journal,* April 17, 1742).

Christopher Hogwood
Cambridge, England
July 1991

Vidimus Enim Stellam Eius in Oriente

GEORGE FRIDERIC HANDEL

Messiah

A SACRED ORATORIO

Majora canamus.

And without Controversy, great is the Mystery of Godliness: God was manifested in the Flesh, justify'd by the Spirit, seen of Angels, preached among the Gentiles, believed on in the World, received up in glory.

In whom are hid all the Treasures of Wisdom and Knowledge.

Comfort Ye My People

Part One.

I

RECITATIVE, ACCOMPANIED: Comfort ye, comfort ye
my People, saith your God; speak ye comfortably to
Jerusalem, and cry unto her, that her Warfare is
accomplished, that her Iniquity is pardon'd.

Isaiah 40: 1–3

The Voice of him that crieth in the Wilderness, Prepare
ye the Way of the Lord, make straight in the Desert a
Highway for our God.

SONG: Every Valley shall be exalted, and every Mountain
and Hill made low, the Crooked straight, and the rough
Places plain.

Isaiah 40: 4

He Is Like a Refiner's Fire

CHORUS: *And the Glory of the Lord shall be revealed, and all*   *Isaiah* 40 : 5
Flesh shall see it together; for the Mouth of the Lord hath
spoken it.

II

RECITATIVE, ACCOMPANIED: Thus saith the Lord   *Haggai* 2 : 6–7
of Hosts; Yet once a little while, and I will shake the
Heavens and the Earth; the Sea, and the dry Land:

And I will shake all Nations; and the Desire of all
Nations shall come.

The Lord whom ye seek shall suddenly come to his Temple,   *Malachi* 3 : 1
even the Messenger of the Covenant, whom ye delight
in: Behold He shall come, saith the Lord of Hosts.

SONG: But who may abide the Day of his coming? And who   *Malachi* 3 : 2
shall stand when He appeareth?

For He is like a Refiner's Fire:

CHORUS: *And He shall purify the Sons of Levi, that they*   *Malachi* 3 : 3
may offer unto the Lord an Offering in Righteousness.

A Virgin Shall Conceive

III

RECITATIVE: Behold, a Virgin shall conceive, and bear a
Son, and shall call his Name *Emmanuel*, GOD WITH US.

Isaiah 7 : 14

SONG AND CHORUS: O thou that tellest good Tidings to
Zion, get thee up into the high Mountain: O thou that
tellest good Tidings to *Jerusalem,* lift up thy Voice with
Strength; lift it up, be not afraid: Say unto the Cities of
Judah, Behold your God.

Isaiah
40 : 9, 60 : 1

Arise, shine, for thy Light is come, and the Glory of the
Lord is risen upon thee.

RECITATIVE, ACCOMPANIED: For behold, Darkness
shall cover the Earth, and gross Darkness the People; but
the Lord shall arise upon thee, and his Glory shall be
seen upon thee.

Isaiah 60 : 2–3

And the *Gentiles* shall come to thy Light, and Kings to
the Brightness of thy Rising.

SONG: The People that walked in Darkness have seen a great
Light; they that dwell in the Land of the Shadow of
Death, upon them hath the Light shined.

Isaiah 9 : 2

There Were Shepherds Abiding in the Field

CHORUS: *For unto us a Child is born, unto us a Son is given;* Isaiah 9 : 6
and the Government shall be upon his Shoulder; and his
Name shall be called Wonderful, Counsellor, The Mighty
God, The Everlasting Father, The Prince of Peace.

IV

RECITATIVE: There were Shepherds abiding in the Field, *Luke 2 : 8*
keeping Watch over their Flock by Night.

RECITATIVE, ACCOMPANIED: And lo, the Angel of the *Luke 2 : 9*
Lord came upon them, and the Glory of the Lord shone
round about them, and they were sore afraid.

RECITATIVE: And the Angel said unto them, Fear not; for *Luke 2 : 10–11*
behold, I bring you good Tidings of great Joy, which shall
be to all People:

For unto you is born this Day, in the City of *David,* a
Saviour, which is Christ the Lord.

RECITATIVE, ACCOMPANIED: And suddenly there was *Luke 2 : 13*
with the Angel a Multitude of the heavenly Host, praising
God, and saying,

The Angel of the Lord

CHORUS: *Glory to God in the Highest, and Peace on Earth,*   *Luke* 2 : 14
Good Will towards Men.

V

SONG: Rejoice greatly, O Daughter of *Sion*, shout,   *Zechariah* 9 : 9–10
O Daughter of *Jerusalem;* behold thy King cometh unto
thee: He is the righteous Saviour; and He shall speak
Peace unto the Heathen.

RECITATIVE: Then shall the Eyes of the Blind be open'd,   *Isaiah* 35 : 5–6
and the Ears of the Deaf unstopped; then shall the lame
Man leap as a Hart, and the Tongue of the Dumb shall
sing.

SONG: He shall feed his Flock like a Shepherd: He shall   *Isaiah* 40 : 11
gather the Lambs with his Arm, and carry them in his
Bosom, and gently lead those that are with young.

Come unto Him all ye that labour and are heavy laden,   *Matthew* 11 : 28
and He will give you Rest.

He Shall Gather the Lambs with His Arm

Take his Yoke upon you, and learn of Him; for He is *Matthew* 11: 29
meek and lowly in Heart: and ye shall find Rest unto your
Souls.

CHORUS: *His Yoke is easy, and his Burthen is light.* *Matthew* 11: 30

The End of the FIRST PART.

Behold the Lamb of God

Part Two.

I

CHORUS: *Behold the Lamb of God, that taketh away the Sin of the World!*

John 1: 29

SONG: He was despised and rejected of Men, a Man of Sorrows, and acquainted with Grief.

Isaiah 53: 3, 50: 6

He gave his Back to the Smiters, and his Cheeks to them that plucked off the Hair: He hid not his Face from Shame and Spitting.

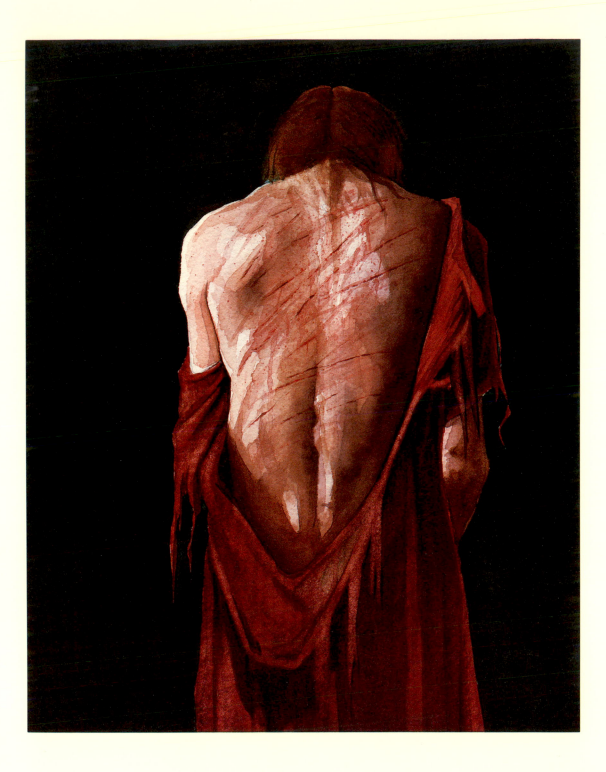

And With His Stripes We Are Healed

CHORUS: *Surely He hath borne our Griefs, and carried our Sorrows:*

He was wounded for our Transgressions, He was bruised for our Iniquities; the Chastisement of our Peace was upon Him

CHORUS: *and with His Stripes we are healed.*

CHORUS: *All we, like Sheep, have gone astray, we have turned every one to his own Way, and the Lord hath laid on Him the Iniquity of us all.*

Isaiah 53: 4–6

RECITATIVE, ACCOMPANIED: All they that see him laugh him to scorn; they shoot out their Lips, and shake their Heads, saying,

Psalm 22: 7

CHORUS: *He trusted in God, that He would deliver him: Let him deliver him, if he delight in him.*

Psalm 22: 8

RECITATIVE, ACCOMPANIED: Thy Rebuke hath broken his Heart; He is full of Heaviness: He looked for some to have Pity on him, but there was no Man, neither found he any to comfort him.

Psalm 69: 20

See, If There Be Any Sorrow Like Unto His Sorrow

SONG: Behold, and see, if there be any Sorrow like unto His Sorrow! *Lamentations 1: 12*

II

RECITATIVE, ACCOMPANIED: He was cut off out of the Land of the Living: For the Transgression of thy People was He Stricken. *Isaiah 53: 8*

SONG: But Thou didst not leave his Soul in Hell, nor didst Thou suffer thy Holy One to see Corruption. *Psalm 16: 10*

III

CHORUS: *Lift up your Heads, O ye Gates, and be ye lift up, ye everlasting Doors, and the King of Glory shall come in.* *Psalm 24: 7–10*

CHORUS: *Who is this King of Glory?*

CHORUS: *The Lord Strong and Mighty; the Lord Mighty in Battle.*

Neither Found He Any to Comfort Him

CHORUS: *Lift up your Heads, O ye Gates, and be ye lift up,*
ye everlasting Doors, and the King of Glory shall come in.

CHORUS: *Who is this King of Glory?*

CHORUS: *The Lord of Hosts: He is the King of Glory.*

IV

RECITATIVE: Unto which of the Angels said He at any time,
Thou art my Son, this Day have I begotten thee?   *Hebrews* 1: 5

CHORUS: *Let all the Angels of God worship Him.*   *Hebrews* 1: 6

V

SONG: Thou art gone up on High; Thou hast led Captivity   *Psalm* 68: 18
captive, and received Gifts for Men, yea, even for thine
Enemies, that the Lord God might dwell among them.

CHORUS: *The Lord gave the Word: Great was the Company*   *Psalm* 68: 11
of the Preachers.

Why Do the Nations So Furiously Rage Together

SONG: How beautiful are the Feet of them that preach the Gospel of Peace, and bring glad Tidings of good Things.

Romans 10 : 15

CHORUS: *Their Sound is gone out into all Lands, and their Words unto the Ends of the World.*

Romans 10 : 18

VI

SONG: Why do the Nations so furiously rage together? and why do the People imagine a vain Thing?

Psalm 2 : 1–2

The Kings of the Earth rise up, and the Rulers take Counsel together against the Lord and against his Anointed.

CHORUS: *Let us break their Bonds asunder, and cast away their Yokes from us.*

Psalm 2 : 3

VII

RECITATIVE: He that dwelleth in Heaven shall laugh them to scorn; the Lord shall have them in Derision.

Psalm 2 : 4

Hallelujah!

SONG: Thou shalt break them with a Rod of Iron; Thou shalt *Psalm* 2 : 9
dash them in pieces like a Potter's Vessel.

VIII

CHORUS: *Hallelujah! for the Lord God Omnipotent reigneth.* *Revelation* 19 : 6

The Kingdom of this World is become the Kingdom of our *Revelation* 11 : 15, 19 : 16
Lord and of his Christ; and He shall reign for ever and
ever, King of Kings, and Lord of Lords. Hallelujah!

The End of the SECOND PART.

Sanctus Spiritus

Part Three.

I

SONG: I Know that my Redeemer liveth, and that He shall   *Job* 19 : 25-26
stand at the latter Day upon the Earth:

And tho' Worms destroy this Body, yet in my Flesh shall I
see God.

For now is Christ risen from the Dead, the First–Fruits   *1 Corinthians* 15 : 20
of them that sleep.

CHORUS: *Since by Man came Death, by Man came also*   *1 Corinthians* 15 : 21–22
the Resurrection of the Dead.

For as in Adam *all die, even so in* Christ *shall all be*
made alive.

The Trumpet Shall Sound

II

RECITATIVE, ACCOMPANIED: Behold, I tell you a
    Mystery: We shall not all sleep, but we shall all be
    changed, in a Moment, in the Twinkling of an Eye,
    at the last Trumpet.

1 Corinthians 15 : 51–52

SONG: The Trumpet shall sound, and the Dead shall be
    raised incorruptible, and We shall be changed.

1 Corinthians 15 : 52–53

For this Corruptible must put on Incorruption, and this
Mortal must put on Immortality.

III

RECITATIVE: Then shall be brought to pass the Saying that
    is written; Death is swallow'd up in Victory.

1 Corinthians 15 : 54

DUET: O Death, where is thy Sting? O Grave, where is thy
    Victory?

1 Corinthians 15 : 55–56

The Sting of Death is Sin, and the Strength of Sin is the
Law.

Dignus Est Agnus

CHORUS: *But Thanks be to God, who giveth Us the Victory through our Lord Jesus Christ.*   *1 Corinthians 15:57*

SONG: If God be for us, who can be against us?   *Romans 8:31, 33–34*

Who shall lay any thing to the Charge of God's Elect? It is God that justifieth; who is he that condemneth?

It is Christ that died, yea, rather that is risen again; who is at the Right Hand of God; who maketh Intercession for us.

IV

CHORUS: *Worthy is the Lamb that was slain, and hath redeemed us to God by his Blood, to receive Power, and Riches, and Wisdom, and Strength, and Honour, and Glory, and Blessing.*   *Revelation 5:9, 12–14*

Blessing, and Honour, Glory, and Power, be unto Him that sitteth upon the Throne, and unto the Lamb, for ever and ever. Amen.

FINIS.

AFTERWORD

MOST OF THE IMAGES HEREIN SPEAK FOR THEMSELVES AND NEED NO FURTHER ILLUMINATION. Those that utilize emblems and symbols, however, may need some elucidation for readers who are unfamiliar with them. For instance, the three images that face each of the three part openings bear emblems of the Godhead.

Opposite the first part opening is the "yod"—the first letter of the Hebrew word for God, *Yahweh,* frequently used as a symbol of God the Father in Christian symbolism. Facing the opening of the second part is a latinized monogram for God the Son, IHC, which is fashioned from the iota, eta, and sigma of the Greek form of the name Jesus. Part three opens opposite an emblem of God the Holy Spirit, the two S's standing for the Latin, *Sanctus Spiritus.* The INRI, which is posted above the head of the crucified Christ, is comprised of the first letters of the Latin phrase *Iesus Nazarenus Rex Iudaeorum,* which means "Jesus of Nazareth, King of the Jews." It is interesting to note that this "charge" was also written in Hebrew and Greek, the two other languages in common usage at that time and place. Peter Paul Rubens's painting of the Crucifixion shows it fully spelled out in all three languages.

The Chi-Rho, which faces the opening of the introduction, is the oldest Christogram (set of letters referring to Christ) and is formed from the first two letters (chi and rho) of the Greek name of Christ: XPICTOC (CHRISTOS).

The captions for the first and last paintings in this book are given in Latin, and I offer translations. The title of the first, *Vidimus enim stellam eius in oriente,* are the words of the Magi, which translate, "We have seen his star in the east." The caption of the final painting, *Dignus est Agnus,* is the Latin for the first phrase of Handel's final chorus, "Worthy Is the Lamb." The banner bearing the red cross, by the way, is a symbol of the Resurrection, often depicted being carried by the Risen Christ.

Barry Moser
Bear Run
May 1991

FOR FURTHER READING

Burrows, Donald, *Handel: Messiah*. Cambridge Music Handbooks, Cambridge University Press, 1991; Dean, Winton, *Handel's Dramatic Oratorios and Masques*. Oxford University Press, pb 1990; Hogwood, Christopher, *Handel*. Thames & Hudson, pb 1988; Larsen, Jens Peter, *Handel's Messiah*. Norton, pb 1990; Sadie, Stanley, *Handel*. Riverrun Press, pb 1985; Shaw, Watkins, *The Story of Handel's Messiah*. London: Novello, 1963; Shaw, Watkins, *A Textual and Historical Companion to Handel's Messiah*. London: Novello, 1965.

MUSICAL SCORES

Vocal and full scores published by Novello & Co. (edited by Watkins Shaw, 1965) and Edition Peters (edited by Donald Burrows, 1987). A facsimile of Handel's conducting score (the "Tenbury" score) is published by The Scolar Press (1974).

The paintings in this book were executed in transparent watercolor on paper handmade by Simon Green at the Barcham Green Mills, Maidstone, Kent, Great Britain.
The calligraphy is the work of Reassurance Wunder.
The text type was composed in Jan Tschichold's Sabon by Cardinal Type, New York, New York.
The transparencies were made by Gamma One Conversions, New York, New York.
The separations were made by Imago Ltd., Hong Kong.
The jacket was printed by Phoenix Color Corp. in Long Island City, New York.
The interior was printed and bound by Worzalla Publishing Company, Stevens Point, Wisconsin.
Production by John Vitale and Danielle Valentino
Designed by Barry Moser and Al Cetta